Been There!
SPAIN

Annabel Savery

W
FRANKLIN WATTS
LONDON • SYDNEY

Facts about Spain

Population: 40 million

Capital city: Madrid

Currency: Euro (€)

Main language: Spanish

Rivers: Guadalquivir, Ebro, Duero, Tajo

Area: 505,988 square kilometres (195,363 square miles)

An Appleseed Editions book

Paperback edition 2014

First published in 2011 by Franklin Watts
338 Euston Road, London NW1 3BH

Franklin Watts Australia
Level 17/207 Kent St, Sydney, NSW 2000

© 2011 Appleseed Editions

Created by Appleseed Editions Ltd,
Well House, Friars Hill, Guestling, East Sussex TN35 4ET

Planning and production by Discovery Books Limited
www.discoverybooks.net
Designed by Ian Winton
Edited by Annabel Savery
Map artwork by Stefan Chabluk
Picture research by Tom Humphrey

ISBN 978 1 4451 3292 1

Dewey Classification: 946'.083

A CIP catalogue for this book is available from the British Library.

Picture Credits: Corbis: p7 bottom (Peter Adams / JAI), p19 (Dallas and John Heaton), p21 (Karl Foersterling), pp22-23
(Michelle Chaplow), p25 bottom (Guido Cozzi), p27 top (Jean-Pierry Lescourret), p29 main (Francesc Muntada); Discovery
Photo Library: p12 (Chris Fairclough); Getty Images: p5 top & p31 (Raul Touzon), p6 (Luis Castanedc Inc.), p7 top (Travel Inc.),
p10 (Jupiter Images), p13 (Michael Busselle), p14 & p30 (Chris Rennie), pp16-17 (Marco Cristofori), p18 bottom (Marwan
Naamani), p26 (Cristina Quicler / Stringer), p28 (DEA / W. Buss); Istockphoto: p8 (Graham Heywood), p18 top (dtimiraos), p29
inset (Juanmonino); Shutterstock: title & p24 (S. Borisov), p2 (Alexander Zavadsky), p5 middle (Olga Ekaterincheva), p9 middle
(Rafael Ramirez Lee), p9 bottom (rubiphoto), p11 top & p30 (Dominique Landau), p11 bottom (viki2win), p15 (sbego), p20 &
p31(Oscar Garry), p23 inset (Alexander Inglessi), p25 top (Brian Maudsley), p27 bottom (absolute); WikiMedia: p9 top (Aleph).

Cover photos: (Hervé Hughes/Hemis); Shutterstock: main (SOMATUSCAN), left (nito).

Printed in Singapore.

Franklin Watts is a division of Hachette Children's Books, an Hachette UK company.
www.hachette.co.uk

Contents

Off to Spain!

We are going on holiday to Spain. This is a big country in the continent of Europe.

Spain is on an area of land that is almost completely surrounded by water. This is called the Iberian Peninsula.

Atlantic Ocean

BASQUE COUNTRY

0 — 200 kilometres

0 — 200 miles

Bilbao

FRANCE

ANDORRA

Pyrenees

Santiago de Compostela

Nervión River

Brolo

Duero River

Ebro River

Barcelona

PORTUGAL

Madrid

Tajo River

SPAIN

Valencia

BALEARIC ISLANDS

Seville

Guadalquivir River

Granada

Mediterranean Sea

N
W E
S

Atlantic Ocean

GIBRALTAR

ALCERIA

Flamenco dancer

Spain has a long coastline, so there are many beaches. There are areas of mountains and forests too.

Mum says we have to pack clothes for warm and cold weather as the **climate** can vary from place to place. I hope it is nice and hot.

Here are some things I know about Spain...

- Flamenco is a traditional Spanish dance.
- Fruits such as oranges are grown in Spain. Many of them are sold to other countries.
- Lots of people go on holiday to Spain every year. Many go for the hot weather and beautiful beaches.

On our trip I'm going to find out lots more!

As we fly over Spain I look out of the aeroplane window. I can see cities, towns and villages down below. There are hills, rivers and farmland, too.

We land in Madrid at lunchtime. This is the hottest time of the day. Many people have a long break in the middle of the day called a **siesta**.

Madrid is the capital city of Spain. On the way to the hotel we see big buildings and open squares, with statues and fountains.

Spanish people often start work early in the morning. At noon they have lunch and then a siesta, then they go back to work. Dinner is often not eaten until ten o'clock in the evening.

A day in the capital

The next day we get up early to explore before it gets too hot. Madrid is noisy and bustling with people and cars.

First, we are going to visit the *Palacio Real* or Royal Palace. Spain has had different types of rulers. Today, there is a king and a government.

The *Palacio Real* is huge. There are 2,800 rooms and 23 courtyards. I am exhausted when we leave, and ready for a siesta.

The King of Spain is called Juan Carlos I. He does not live in the *Palacio Real* but has a smaller palace outside the city called the *Zarzuela Palace*.

In the afternoon we go to the Prado Museum. This museum is full of famous works of art.

I like looking at the paintings. Many of them are by Spanish artists.

A shopping trip

Spanish people like to shop at markets. Some stalls are piled high with brightly coloured fruit and vegetables. Others are selling sausages, olives or cheeses.

Mum says that nearly all the food is grown by farmers in Spain. Farming is very important here.

Sheep and pigs are raised for meat. Crops are grown in central Spain where there are big, open areas of land. Around the coasts, orange and lemon trees are planted. In the south there are many olive trees, growing in long lines (below).

Did you know that Spain is the world's leading producer of olive oil? There are more than 300 million olive trees and Spain produces more than a million tonnes of olive oil each year.

Green Galicia

From Madrid we fly to Santiago de Compostela. This is a city is in the north-west corner of Spain, in a region called Galicia.

The city has a huge cathedral. Dad takes us inside to see the **tomb** of Saint James.

Each year many Catholics travel a long way to visit the cathedral. A long religious journey like this is called a pilgrimage. Roman Catholicism is the main religion in Spain.

From Galicia we travel across the north coast. The land here is green and there are lots of forests. The north coast is known as the *Costa Verde*. *Verde* means 'green' in Spanish.

Finally, we arrive in the Basque country.

The Basque country

The Basque country is a region in the north-east of Spain. Dad says this region has a different history and **culture** from the rest of Spain.

The biggest city here is Bilbao. The River Nervión runs through the city to the sea. On the coast is the busy Bilbao port.

One of the most famous buildings in Bilbao is the *Museo Guggenheim*. It is bright silver and there are lots of parts sticking up at different angles. It is very interesting to look at.

The people in the Basque country have their own language called Euskera. This is a very unusual language because it is different from any other language in the world.

In the Pyrenees

France and Spain are separated by a range of mountains called the Pyrenees.

We are going to stay in a small village in the Pyrenean **foothills** called Brolo. From here the hills get higher and higher until they turn into mountains. Many people come here to walk or to ski.

The village is quiet. Many people have moved from small villages to cities like Barcelona and Madrid to look for jobs.

From the village we take a picnic and go for a long walk. Snow-capped mountains are far ahead of us and there are green valleys to look down into.

Busy in Barcelona

Now we are going by bus to Barcelona. This is a big city on the east coast. It is hotter here than in the mountains.

We stay in a hotel near the city centre. For breakfast we have hot chocolate and *churros*. Churros (right) are long sticks of deep-fried sweet dough. Yum!

Barcelona has one of the top football teams in Europe. In 2009 they won the FIFA Club World Cup.

Dad takes us to a church called the *Sagrada Familia*. He says that a famous Spanish **architect** called Antonio Gaudi designed it. There are lots of **spires** and it is decorated all over.

Most people here speak Catalan. This is an old language spoken in north-east Spain and parts of France, Andorra and Italy too.

From Barcelona, we travel further down the east coast to Valencia. We are staying in a villa there.

The villa owner is called Maria. She tells us that the best thing about Valencia is the *Las Fallas* fiesta in March. *Fiesta* means 'festival'.

The fiesta celebrates Saint Joseph's Day. Saint Joseph is the **patron saint** of carpenters. Tall papier-maché statues are built and on the last day of the festival they are burnt in the streets.

Each city, town and village in Spain has its own fiestas. Some go on for as long as a week.

Near Valencia in the town of Buñol there is a fiesta called La Tomatina. For three hours people throw tomatoes at each other!

Along the coast

From Valencia we are going to travel south along the coast. There are many beaches and the sea looks lovely and blue.

All the areas along the coast of Spain have names. *Costa Blanca* means the 'white coast' and *Costa del Sol* means 'coast of the sun'.

The beaches are packed. People are sunbathing and swimming in the sea. Lots of people come to the coast for their holidays.

In the evening we go to a restaurant. Most of the restaurants have outside tables. People stroll past while we have our meal.

For dinner we have paella. This is a very popular dish here. It is a stew made with rice, saffron, meat, fish and shellfish. It's delicious.

Exploring Granada

Next, we drive inland to Granada.

In the morning we go to see the Alhambra Palace. It is perched on top of a hill above the city.

The Alhambra Palace was built by people called the Moors. The Moors came from North Africa. They invaded Spain more than 1,400 years ago and built great forts and cities.

Every part of the palace is decorated with beautiful patterns. Inside, there are open courtyards with green plants and pools of water.

In the evening we go to see a flamenco show. The women dancers twirl around, moving their arms and stamping their feet. A man plays a guitar and sings too. The audience clap their hands to keep the rhythm.

From Granada we travel to Seville. On the way we visit the Doñana National Park. This is a big area of **wetland**. The park is a protected area because lots of wild animals and plants are found here.

We arrive in Seville in the evening and go for a stroll. It is a very old city with narrow, winding streets. Many houses are white; others are painted bright colours.

The next day we go to see the *Plaza de Toros de la Maestranza*, a famous bullfighting ring. It is a big, white, circular building with a grand entrance. Inside there are lots of seats around a main ring.

In Spanish, bullfights are called *corridas*. At a *corrida* a man called a *matador* fights a bull. It is a very old Spanish sport, but it is still popular with people today.

Castle country

We journey back to Madrid on a high-speed train. On the way we are going to go through the region of *Castilla la Mancha*.

Dad says that this region is famous for its castles. Many people have fought over who should rule Spain and each built castles to protect their territory. There are over 3,000 castles in Spain.

A lot of the land that we pass is being used for farming. Many farmers raise sheep here. They use sheep's milk to make a cheese called *manchego*.

The high-speed train really whizzes along! It only takes a couple of hours to travel the 400 kilometres (250 miles) to Madrid.

We are going to fly home from Madrid. On the plane home we make a list of our favourite things about Spain. I liked the flamenco dancing best.

Buenos dias
(*say* **Bway-nohs dee-ahs**) Hello / Good Morning

Adios (*say* **Ah-dee-ohs**) Goodbye

Como estás?
(*say* **Koh-moh ay-stahs**) How are you?

Como te llamas?
(*say* **Koh-moh tay yah-mahs**) What is your name?

Me llamo Helen.
(*say* **May yah-moh Helen**) My name is Helen.

Counting 1-10

1 **uno**　2 **dos**　3 **tres**　4 **cuatro**

5 **cinco**　6 **seis**　7 **siete**　8 **ocho**

9 **nueve**　10 **diez**

Words to remember

architect a person who designs buildings

climate the usual weather in a place

culture the ideas, customs and art of a particular place

foothills the lower hills near the base of a mountain or group of mountains

patron saint a saint who is regarded as the particular guardian of a country, church, trade or person

siesta an afternoon nap or rest

spire the pointed structure on top of a building

tomb a grave for an important person

wetland land with many marshes and swamps

Index

Learning more about Spain

Books

Spain (Country Topics) M Bougard, Franklin Watts, 2007.
Spain (Discover Countries) Paul Harrison, Wayland, 2009.
Spain (Facts about Countries) Ian Graham, Franklin Watts, 2005.
Spain (Find out about) Duncan Cosbie, Franklin Watts, 2007.
Take your Camera to Spain Ted Park, Raintree, 2004.

Websites

National Geographic Kids, People and places
   http://kids.nationalgeographic.com/places/find/spain
Geography for kids, Geography online and Geography games
   http://www.kidsgeo.com/index.php
SuperKids Geography directory, lots of sites to help with geography learning.
   http://www.super-kids.com/geography.html